A Girl Named Rebekah
The Story of God's Answer to Abraham

We are grateful to the following team of authors for their contributions to *God Loves Me*, a Bible story program for young children. This Bible story, one of a series of fifty-two, was written by Patricia L. Nederveld, managing editor for CRC Publications. Suggestions for using this book were developed by Sherry Ten Clay, training coordinator for CRC Publications and freelance author from Albuquerque, New Mexico. Yvonne Van Ee, an early childhood educator, served as project consultant and wrote *God Loves Me*, the program guide that accompanies this series of Bible storybooks.

Nederveld has served as a consultant to Title I early childhood programs in Colorado. She has extensive experience as a writer, teacher, and consultant for federally funded preschool, kindergarten, and early childhood programs in Colorado, Texas, Michigan, Florida, Missouri, and Washington, using the High/Scope Education Research Foundation curriculum. In addition to writing the Bible Footprints church school curriculum for four- and five-year-olds, Nederveld edited the revised *Threes* curriculum and the first edition of preschool through second grade materials for the *LiFE* curriculum, all published by CRC Publications.

Ten Clay taught preschool for ten years in public schools in California, Missouri, and North Carolina and served as a Title IV preschool teacher consultant in Kansas City. For over twenty-five years she has served as a church preschool leader and also as a MOPS (Mothers of Preschoolers) volunteer. Ten Clay is coauthor of the preschool-kindergarten materials of the *LiFE* curriculum published by CRC Publications.

Van Ee is a professor and early childhood program advisor in the Education Department at Calvin College, Grand Rapids, Michigan. She has served as curriculum author and consultant for Christian Schools International and wrote the original *Story Hour* organization manual and curriculum materials for fours and fives.

Photo on page 5: Paul Barton/Stock Market; photo on page 20: SuperStock.

© 1998 by CRC Publications, 2850 Kalamazoo Ave. SE, Grand Rapids, MI 49560. All rights reserved. With the exception of brief excerpts for review purposes, no part of this book may be reproduced in any manner whatsoever without written permission from the publisher. Printed in the United States of America on recycled paper. ♻ 1-800-333-8300

Library of Congress Cataloging-in-Publication Data

Nederveld, Patricia L., 1944-
    A girl named Rebekah: the story of God's answer to Abraham/
Patricia L. Nederveld.
       p. cm. — (God loves me; bk. 8)
    Summary: A simply retelling of the story of how God answered Abraham's prayer for a suitable wife for his son Isaac. Includes follow-up activities.
      ISBN 1-56212-277-0
     1. Rebekah (Biblical matriarch)—Juvenile literature. 2. Abraham (Biblical patriarch)—Juvenile literature. 3. Bible stories, English—O.T. Genesis.
[1. Abraham (Biblical patriarch) 2. Rebekah (Biblical matriarch) 3. Bible stories—O.T.] I. Title. II. Series: Nederveld, Patricia L., 1944-
God loves me; bk. 8.
BS580.R4N43 1998
222'.1109505—dc21
                                        97-37041
                                            CIP
                                             AC

10 9 8 7 6 5 4 3 2 1

A Girl Named Rebekah
The Story of God's Answer to Abraham

PATRICIA L. NEDERVELD

ILLUSTRATIONS BY LISA WORKMAN

CRC Publications
Grand Rapids, Michigan

This is a story from God's book, the Bible.

It's for *say name(s) of your child(ren).* It's for me too!

Genesis 24

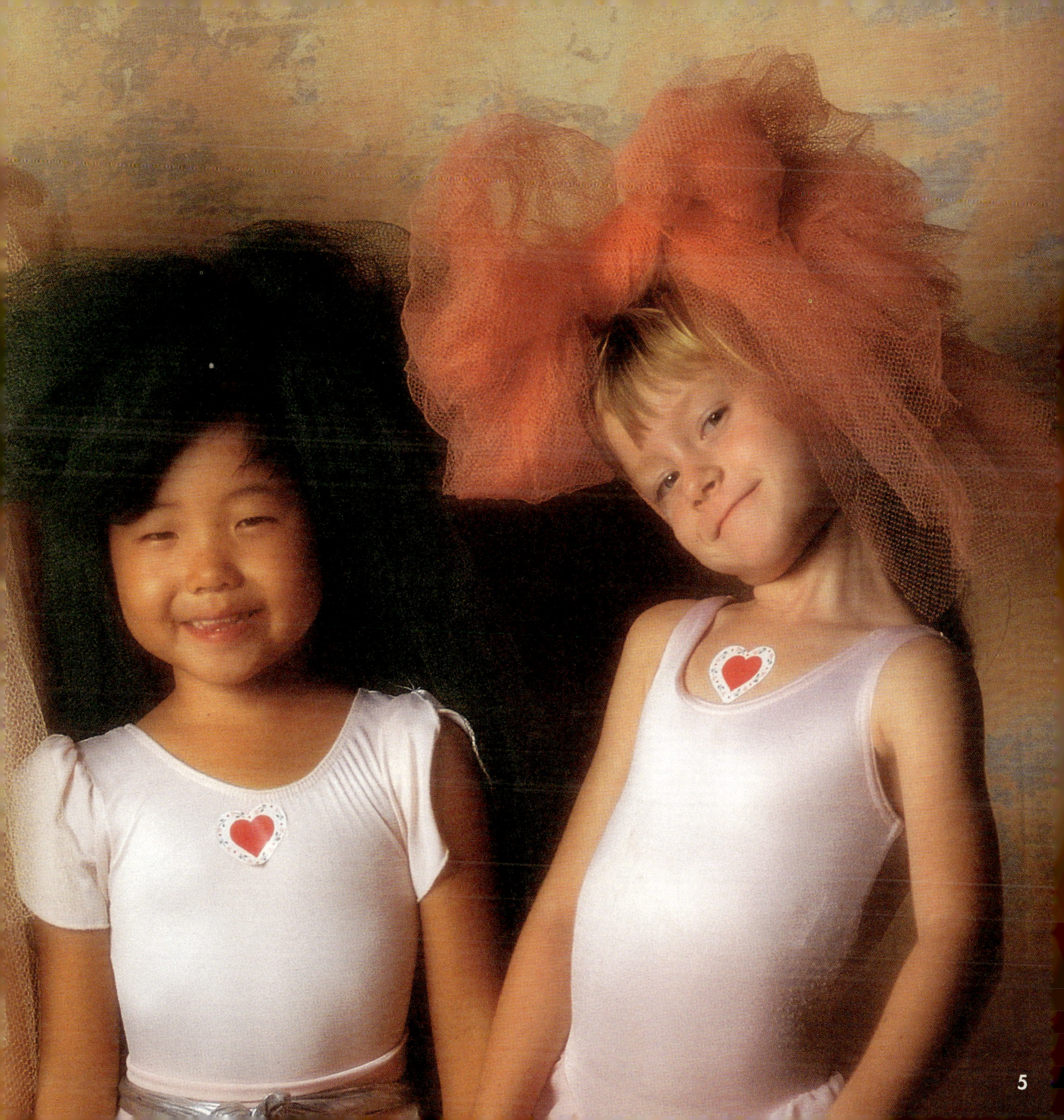

Once there was a family God loved very much. Abraham and Sarah and their son, Isaac, loved God very much too.

7

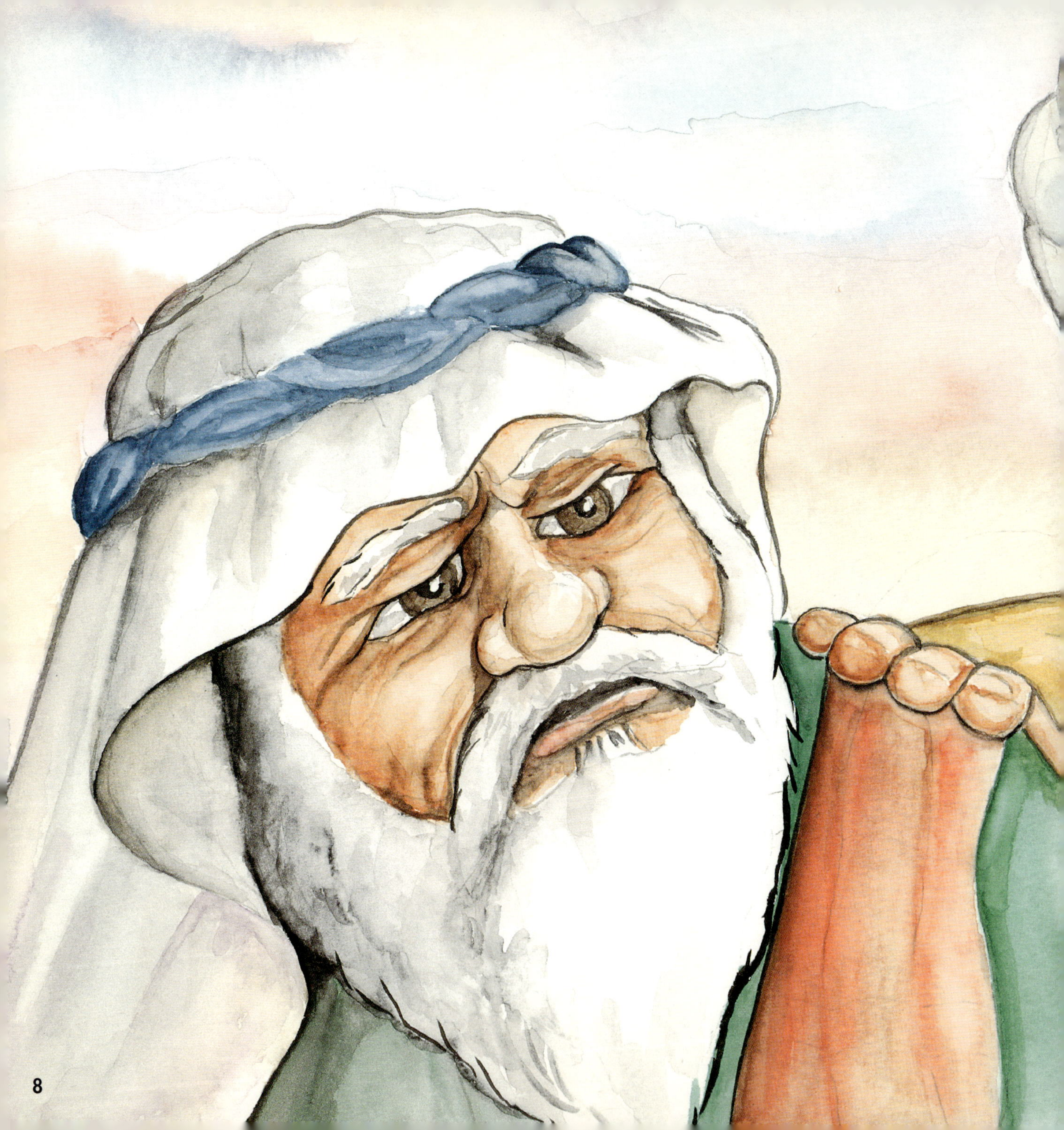

When Mother Sarah died, Father Abraham felt sad. He was worried too. It was time for Isaac to find someone to marry—someone who loved God.

Abraham talked to his helper, Eliezer. "My son needs to marry a woman who loves God. Will you help me find her?"

"Yes, I'll go!" Eliezer promised. "I'll find someone for Isaac—someone who loves God."

"God will go with you," said Abraham.

Eliezer traveled far. One day, when the sun was hot overhead, Eliezer stopped for a drink of water. "Will I find her here?" he wondered.

Eliezer prayed, "Please, dear God, help me find a wife for Isaac. Maybe it could work like this—I'll ask someone for a drink. If she says yes and then gives my camels a drink too, I'll know for sure that she is the one!"

God listened to Eliezer. And God sent Rebekah! When Rebekah filled her jar with water, Eliezer asked her for a drink of water. She gave him a drink—and his thirsty camels too!

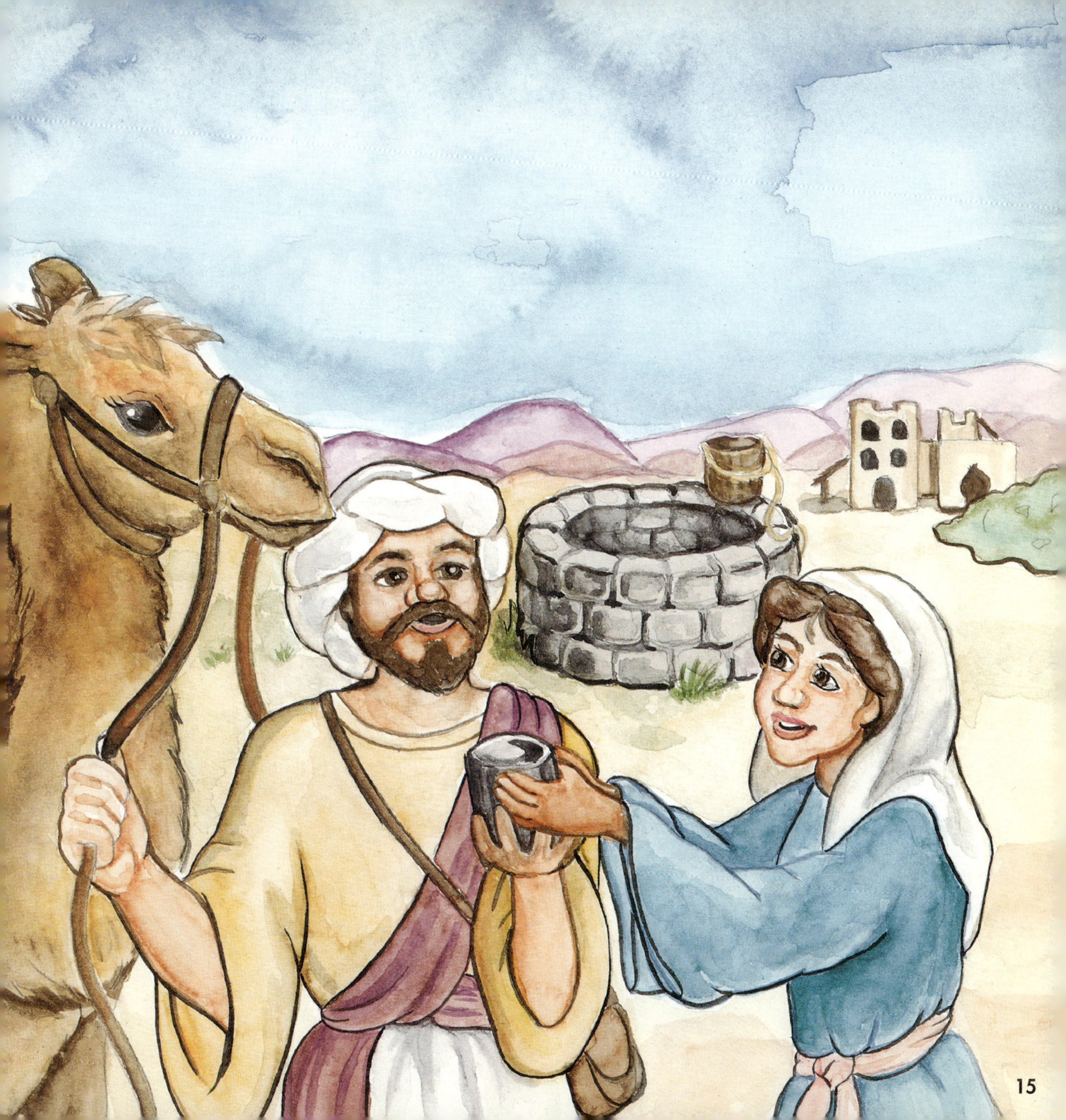

16

Eliezer was excited. He gave Rebekah a present—bracelets and rings. When Rebekah brought Eliezer home, he could see that her family loved God too.

"Will you go with me? Will you be Isaac's wife?" asked Eliezer.

"I will go," answered Rebekah, for she knew that God would always take good care of her.

And that is how Rebekah and Isaac found each other and became a new family. They loved God very much.

19

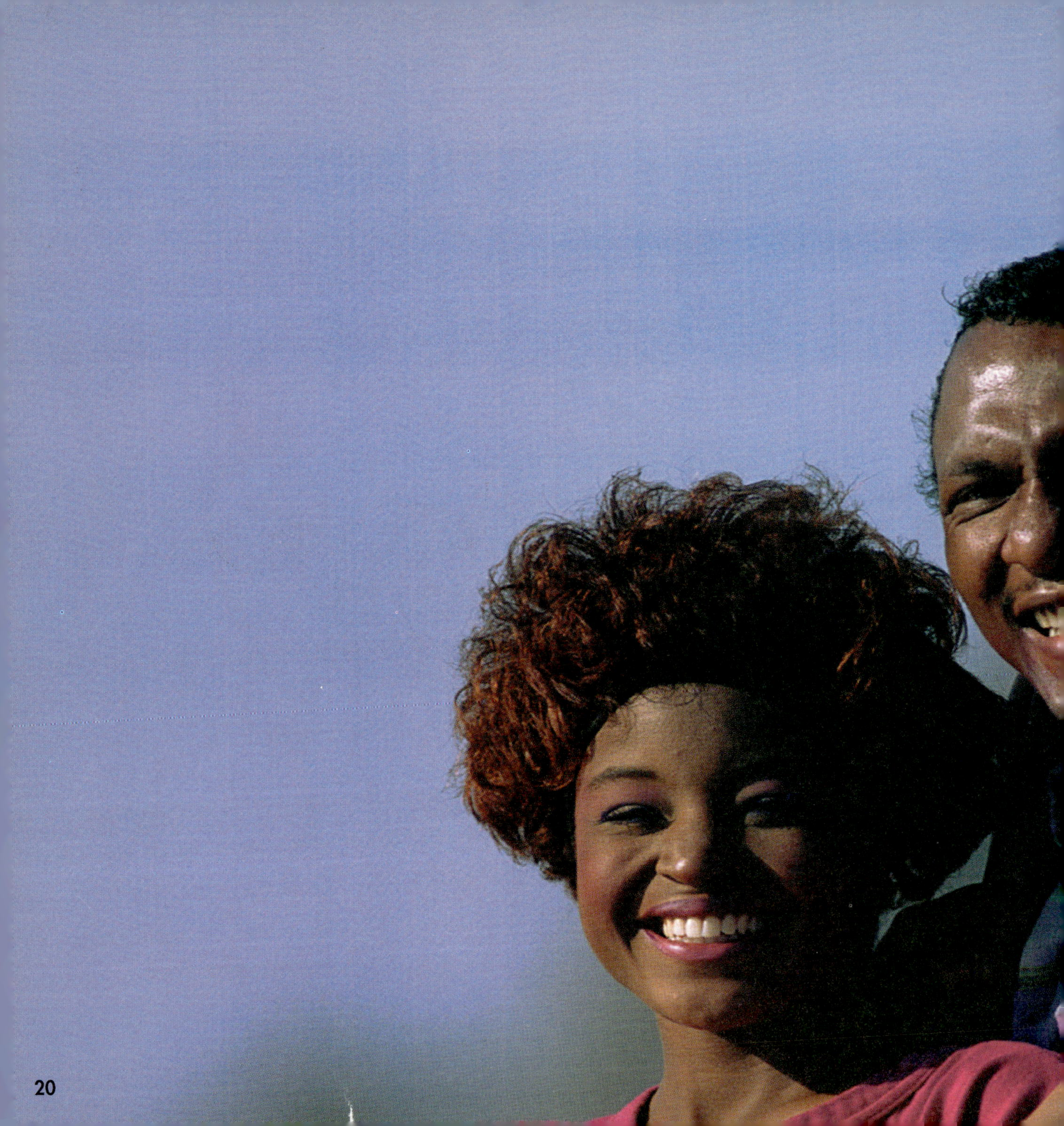

I wonder if you know that God loves *your* family too . . .

Dear God, we're glad that you promise to be our God. Thank you that our families belong to you too. Amen.

Suggestions for Follow-up

Opening

Welcome your children today with a blessing. Call them by name, and tell them how much God loves them. Give each child a gentle hug or soft touch.

As you begin, remind your children that God loves each one—and their families too! Sing "God Is So Good" (Songs Section, *God Loves Me* program guide). You might want to add this new stanza:

God loves me so . . .

Learning Through Play

Learning through play is the best way! The following activity suggestions are meant to help you provide props and experiences that will invite the children to play their way into the Scripture story and its simple truth. Try to provide plenty of time for the children to choose their own activities and to play individually. Use group activities sparingly—little ones learn most comfortably with a minimum of structure.

1. A dress-up box with old wedding veils or squares of lace, blouses, shirts, low-heeled shoes, bracelets, and hats will provide lots of fun. Keep a mirror nearby so your children can see their new costumes. You might want to ask if they are pretending to be different characters in today's story. Or you could just compliment the fashions as you hold up the mirror. Add toy horses or broomsticks to encourage more dramatic play.

2. Enjoy a tasty art project today. Cut 8" (20 cm) lengths of yarn, and wind masking tape in a spiral on one end to create a needle. Set out bowls of any circle cereal to use as beads. When your little one is finished stringing cereal—and tasting too—cut off the masking tape and tie the two ends together to form a bracelet.

3. Take a trip to find Rebekah. Ask a teenager to play the part of Rebekah and an older adult male to play the part of Eliezer. Provide simple costumes if you wish. Station Rebecca in a "far-away" place inside or outside. To keep your little ones safe, use a long jump rope as a walking rope. Let Eliezer take the rope at one end, and show children how to hold onto the rope with one hand as you bring up the rear.

   As you walk, wonder together where you will find someone for Isaac to love. When you find Rebekah, enjoy a drink of water (provide a pitcher and paper cups for Rebekah). Perhaps your Rebckah will want to tell your little ones how much she loves God.

4. Spread colored pipe cleaners out on a table or blanket. Make rings or bracelets. Talk about the story while you work. Remember to share your own excitement that God loves you and your family.

5. Invite children to take turns being Rebekah. Rebekah can hide while the other children cover their eyes with their hands. As you hunt for Rebekah, sing this song (tune: "Where Is Thumbkin?"):

Where's Rebekah?
Where's Rebekah?
Here she is.
Here she is.
I'm so glad God loves us.
I'm so glad God loves us.
We love God.

6. On a large sheet of posterboard, write the caption God Loves Families. Bring pictures of babies, young children, teenagers, parents, and grandparents cut from magazines. Invite your little ones to make a great big family collage using glue sticks and the pictures you've brought. Talk about God's love for families—for tiny babies and grandpas and grandmas too. For extra fun, provide heart stickers for children to add to the collage.

7. Ahead of time, cover a gift box with pretty paper so the lid can be removed without ripping the paper. Inside, have a personalized card for each child that says, "God loves [name]." Add heart stickers if you wish. Remember to include a card for yourself too! Send each child home with a card.

Closing
Quietly hum "God Is So Good" (Songs Section, *God Loves Me* program guide), and sing the words again as your little ones help pick up. Gather the children around you and join hands as you pray this prayer: "Thank you, God, for loving us. We love you. Amen."

At Home
Celebrate the fact that God loves your family! Make a favorite meal, and let your little one help with simple chores such as table setting or easy cooking. You might want to make heart-shaped gelatin blocks for a salad and use pretty napkins. At the beginning of your meal, take turns saying, "Thank you, God, for loving me." Sometime during your meal, tell your little one how happy you are that God loves you and that your family belongs to God.

Old Testament Stories

Blue and Green and Purple Too! *The Story of God's Colorful World*
It's a Noisy Place! *The Story of the First Creatures*
Adam and Eve *The Story of the First Man and Woman*
Take Good Care of My World! *The Story of Adam and Eve in the Garden*
A Very Sad Day *The Story of Adam and Eve's Disobedience*
A Rainy, Rainy Day *The Story of Noah*
Count the Stars! *The Story of God's Promise to Abraham and Sarah*
A Girl Named Rebekah *The Story of God's Answer to Abraham*
Two Coats for Joseph *The Story of Young Joseph*
Plenty to Eat *The Story of Joseph and His Brothers*
Safe in a Basket *The Story of Baby Moses*
I'll Do It! *The Story of Moses and the Burning Bush*
Safe at Last! *The Story of Moses and the Red Sea*
What Is It? *The Story of Manna in the Desert*
A Tall Wall *The Story of Jericho*
A Baby for Hannah *The Story of an Answered Prayer*
Samuel, Samuel! *The Story of God's Call to Samuel*
Lions and Bears! *The Story of David the Shepherd Boy*
David and the Giant *The Story of David and Goliath*
A Little Jar of Oil *The Story of Elisha and the Widow*
One, Two, Three, Four, Five, Six, Seven! *The Story of Elisha and Naaman*
A Big Fish Story *The Story of Jonah*
Lions, Lions! *The Story of Daniel*

New Testament Stories

Jesus Is Born! *The Story of Christmas*
Good News! *The Story of the Shepherds*
An Amazing Star! *The Story of the Wise Men*
Waiting, Waiting, Waiting! *The Story of Simeon and Anna*
Who Is This Child? *The Story of Jesus in the Temple*
Follow Me! *The Story of Jesus and His Twelve Helpers*
The Greatest Gift *The Story of Jesus and the Woman at the Well*
A Father's Wish *The Story of Jesus and a Little Boy*
Just Believe! *The Story of Jesus and a Little Girl*
Get Up and Walk! *The Story of Jesus and a Man Who Couldn't Walk*
A Little Lunch *The Story of Jesus and a Hungry Crowd*
A Scary Storm *The Story of Jesus and a Stormy Sea*
Thank You, Jesus! *The Story of Jesus and One Thankful Man*
A Wonderful Sight! *The Story of Jesus and a Man Who Couldn't See*
A Better Thing to Do *The Story of Jesus and Mary and Martha*
A Lost Lamb *The Story of the Good Shepherd*
Come to Me! *The Story of Jesus and the Children*
Have a Great Day! *The Story of Jesus and Zacchaeus*
I Love You, Jesus! *The Story of Mary's Gift to Jesus*
Hosanna! *The Story of Palm Sunday*
The Best Day Ever! *The Story of Easter*
Goodbye—for Now *The Story of Jesus' Return to Heaven*
A Prayer for Peter *The Story of Peter in Prison*
Sad Day, Happy Day! *The Story of Peter ad Dorcas*
A New Friend *The Story of Paul's Conversion*
Over the Wall *The Story of Paul's Escape in a Basket*
A Song in the Night *The Story of Paul and Silas in Prison*
A Ride in the Night *The Story of Paul's Escape on Horseback*
The Shipwreck *The Story of Paul's Rescue at Sea*

Holiday Stories

Selected stories from the New Testament to help you celebrate the Christian year

Jesus Is Born! *The Story of Christmas*
Good News! *The Story of the Shepherds*
An Amazing Star! *The Story of the Wise Men*
Hosanna! *The Story of Palm Sunday*
The Best Day Ever! *The Story of Easter*
Goodbye—for Now *The Story of Jesus' Return to Heaven*

These fifty-two books are the heart of *God Loves Me*, a Bible story program designed for young children. Individual books (or the entire set) and the accompanying program guide *God Loves Me* are available from CRC Publications (1-800-333-8300).